Cambridge Engl
....
Level
Series editor: Ph

Double Cross

Philip Prowse

CAMBRIDGE
UNIVERSITY PRESS

CAMBRIDGE UNIVERSITY PRESS
Cambridge, New York, Melbourne, Madrid, Cape Town, Singapore, São Paulo

Cambridge University Press
The Edinburgh Building, Cambridge CB2 2RU, UK

www.cambridge.org
Information on this title: www.cambridge.org/9780521656177

First published 1999
10th printing 2005

Printed in the United Kingdom at the University Press, Cambridge

A catalogue record for this publication is available from the British Library

ISBN-13 978-0-521-65617-7 paperback
ISBN-10 0-521-65617-6 paperback

Contents

Characters

Monika Lundgren an agent for Swedish Military Intelligence (SMI), Stockholm.

Anders Blom Monika's boss at SMI.

James Chapman an agent for MI5, British Intelligence, in London.

Kurt Carlsson a senior minister in the Swedish Government.

Millham United a football team from London.

Bruce a guitarist and fan of Millham United.

Adolf Vitjord the leader of a right-wing party in South Africa.

Cabinda a passport officer in Maputo, Mozambique.

Amelia Cabinda's wife.

Places in the story

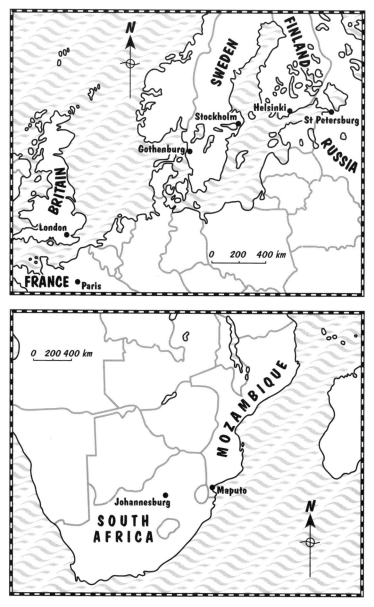

Chapter 1   *Shooting in Stockholm*

The woman standing on the wing of the Boeing Stearman plane was wearing dark glasses. The plane flew under a bridge, and then low over the crowd. The woman waved. The crowd waved back.

It was August 9th. The third day of the Stockholm Water Festival had begun. It was twelve o'clock and today there was a flying show. There were over a hundred thousand people in the centre of Stockholm, Sweden. The roads and squares were full of people, who also stood on the bridges which joined the city's many islands. On the water there were thousands of sailing boats and some larger passenger boats.

A jet plane screamed through the blue summer sky. Everyone looked up. A smaller plane flew over the crowd near the Royal Palace.

Half a kilometre from the Royal Palace a tall blonde woman stood in the crowd outside the City Hall. She was wearing blue shorts and a yellow shirt, and had a yellow bag over her shoulder. The woman's name was Monika Lundgren. She was twenty-six years old. Monika watched the woman on the wing of the Boeing Stearman. It would be an exciting job, she thought. It would also be dangerous, flying high in the clouds and low under bridges. And probably lonely.

'Hey, you!' a man's voice said loudly. Monika turned. A

young man was standing next to her. He was about eighteen. He was wearing red, white and blue shorts. His T-shirt said MAD ABOUT FOOTBALL! His head was shaved and his face was red. He was holding a glass in his hand. He was English and his voice was very loud.

Monika smiled. 'Hello,' she said, and turned away. She looked back at the City Hall. The sun was hot and everyone else was watching the planes.

Monika felt a hand on her arm. She heard a voice. It was the English football fan.

'I said hello,' the fan shouted.

Monika turned again to the young man. She pushed his hand away and stepped back from him. Then she smiled again and turned away. A moment later she felt a hand on her shoulder. The football fan pulled her shoulder and turned her around. Then he pulled her towards him.

'Give me a kiss,' the fan said. 'You're lovely.' He smelt of cigarettes.

A few people in the crowd saw what was happening. But they didn't do anything. Everyone else was watching the planes.

Monika looked into the fan's red eyes. He was holding her with one arm and the glass with the other hand. Monika suddenly put her arms up over her head. The fan's arms flew up in the air and he dropped the glass. Monika was free. She quickly hit the fan hard in the stomach. His head came forward and down as his hands moved to his stomach. There was a look of surprise and pain on his face. Quickly Monika brought her knee up into his face. The fan fell forward. Monika moved behind him. Her right hand held the fan's left arm behind his back, while she put her left hand over his mouth. She moved the fan towards the water. Then Monika kicked him hard from behind. He fell forward into the water. The crowd watched as another jet screamed past in the sky.

Monika looked around, and then walked away from the water. She turned her head left towards her yellow shoulder-bag. She put her mouth near the bag and spoke quietly into it.

An engine started, and from near the City Hall a black boat appeared. The boat went quickly across the water to the football fan. People in the crowd heard the boat and looked towards it. The boat stopped near the fan and two men wearing wet suits pulled the fan into the boat. He was alive and very wet. He was also very angry. He looked at Monika and started to shout something. At that moment one of the men started the engine and the fan's cries were lost. The boat disappeared behind the City Hall. The crowd looked up to the sky again.

Monika Lundgren of the SMI, Sweden's Secret Military Intelligence department, smiled to herself.

'Keep him locked up for the rest of the day, and then let him out,' she said into her shoulder-bag radio.

Then she turned to look at the City Hall. Monika was not there to enjoy the Water Festival. Today she was working with the police. It was important to stop any trouble outside the City Hall.

While the Festival crowds were enjoying the sunshine something much more serious was happening. In the Nobel Prize Room in the City Hall twelve men and women were meeting. They were the leaders of the largest businesses in Europe, North and South America and Asia. The United

Nations had planned the meeting, and the chairman was an important Swedish minister, Kurt Carlsson. He had been the Swedish ambassador in Moscow for three years in the early 1990s. He was forty-five but looked younger. His long brown hair made him look more like a rock star than an ambassador. His voice was loud and clear.

'The former Soviet Union had tens of thousands of nuclear weapons. The Russian army has destroyed some of these weapons already. Destroying a nuclear weapon is dangerous and expensive work. The Russian army would like to destroy many more weapons. But it doesn't have enough money to do so. This is where we must help.'

'But why?' someone asked. 'Why must we help the Russians? They are their nuclear bombs, not ours.'

'It's possible,' Carlsson explained, 'that criminals in the former Soviet Union may steal these nuclear weapons. If these bombs get into the hands of terrorists it would be terrible. The world will only be safe when these weapons are destroyed.'

Carlsson paused for a moment.

No-one around the table said anything. They waited for Carlsson to continue. Then a door opened quietly at the back of the room. A man in a wheelchair moved quickly up to the table and joined the meeting.

'Let me introduce General Anders Blom, of SMI, Swedish Military Intelligence,' said Kurt Carlsson.

Anders Blom had short grey hair and a strong face. He was in his mid-fifties. Twenty years ago someone had shot him while he was working with the United Nations in Africa. The shot had broken his back. Since then he had been in a wheelchair.

Blom looked around the table and smiled. He spoke slowly in a low voice.

'It's really quite simple,' Blom explained. 'Sweden has a very good relationship with the Russian government, and with the other countries of the former Soviet Union. We are ready to help them destroy their nuclear weapons. But they need money to do this – a lot of money. And time is short – we must do something quickly. We know that terrorists are already trying to buy the old Soviet weapons.'

'As Blom says,' Kurt Carlsson continued, 'it is simple. We can help destroy the nuclear weapons, or we can let terrorists get the weapons. And they may destroy the world.'

'What can we do to help?' asked a white-haired Japanese woman. She was the managing director of an international electrical company.

'It will cost one billion American dollars to destroy the weapons,' Blom replied quickly. 'And there is something else. If the Russians destroy their weapons, the USA will follow and destroy theirs.'

'Yes,' Carlsson said. 'And that is why you are here. We want you to give one billion dollars and save the world from nuclear weapons.'

Everyone started to talk at once. It was going to be a long meeting.

Outside the City Hall Monika waited in the sunshine. She watched the crowd. Her job was to make sure that no-one tried to get into the meeting. Time passed, and soon it was three o'clock in the afternoon. The side door of the City Hall opened. Kurt Carlsson, with police all around him, stepped out on to a small platform. Journalists, photographers and TV news reporters stood around the platform. Behind the journalists, some of the Festival crowd watched, a little surprised. People in the boats by the City Hall looked up. Fifty metres out in the water one of Stockholm's old passenger boats slowed down and stopped.

Kurt Carlsson started to speak to the journalists. Monika felt worried. She stood by the platform and looked over the crowd and the water. The sun was shining on the water as Monika looked at the old passenger boat. The name across the front of the boat was SS Vaxholm. There were people standing along the sides of the Vaxholm, looking at the City Hall. There was a sudden, bright light from the boat. Someone taking a photograph, Monika thought.

'Aaaah! Aaaah!' It was Carlsson. His hands were holding his shoulder. Blood ran out from between his fingers. He fell to his knees, and then forward, face down.

Monika's face did not change. She spoke into her shoulder-bag radio. 'Someone has shot Carlsson!' she said quietly.

Chapter 2 *Try and remember exactly what happened*

Blood ran out from under Carlsson's body. Two police officers were on their knees beside him. People in the crowd screamed. Police cars and an ambulance arrived.

Monika remained calm. She was thinking about the few moments before Carlsson fell. The SS Vaxholm had stopped near the City Hall. There had been a sudden light on the boat. Monika hadn't heard anything like a shot. But she had heard something just as Carlsson fell. It was a loud metal sound, like money falling to the ground.

An ambulance took Carlsson to hospital and the police started to clear the crowd away.

Monika walked away from the City Hall. As she went across the Central Bridge she saw the SS Vaxholm disappearing in the distance. The narrow streets of the Old Town were full of tourists. Monika made her way along Stora Nygatan, which means 'the Big New Street', even though it is over six hundred years old, then she turned off into a narrower street. She stopped at a dark doorway, took a plastic card out of her bag and pushed it into a hole in the door. The door opened and Monika went in.

Inside the large old building there was light and lots of activity. This was the offices of the SMI, Swedish Military Intelligence. The shooting of Kurt Carlsson would keep the SMI very busy. Without speaking to anyone, Monika went into her office. Her face looked white and worried.

Someone had tried to kill Carlsson, and she hadn't done anything to stop it.

Monika sat at her desk and looked around her small office. There were two photographs on the desk. Monika picked up one of the photographs and looked at it.

It was a picture of her parents. Monika's mother and father were smiling, and they looked happy. Monika had taken the photo when they were on holiday in Spain, ten years ago.

Soon after their Spanish holiday Monika's parents had died in a car crash. Monika was sixteen at the time of the accident. She had felt terrible and had missed her parents very much. She had gone to live with her grandmother just outside Stockholm. She didn't have any brothers or sisters, and had sometimes been very lonely.

The telephone on her desk rang. It was Blom, her boss.

'I'm in my car on the way back to the office,' he said. 'Carlsson's alive and he's going to be OK.'

'That's good news,' Monika said.

'I want to see you as soon as I get to the office,' Blom continued. 'You were one of the people who were closest to Carlsson when he was shot. Try and remember exactly what happened.'

'Yes, sir,' Monika replied and put down the phone. She felt both happy and angry. Happy because Carlsson was alive. And angry because of Blom's words.

'Try and remember exactly what happened,' Blom had said. He had spoken to her as if she was a child. But she wasn't a child! She was the youngest and the best agent in the SMI!

After her parents' death she had worked hard at school,

and had been very good at languages. She had also been very good at sport. After school Monika had joined the army. Ten months later she had finished her basic training as the best soldier of the year. The army then sent her to the USA, where she trained with American soldiers for a year. She had learnt to parachute and to scuba-dive.

Back in Sweden she was chosen to join the SMI, partly because she spoke Russian and Spanish, as well as Swedish and English, of course. She was sent to South America where she had done difficult and dangerous work for the SMI. While there she had saved the lives of two Swedish tourists who had been kidnapped by terrorists.

Monika picked up the telephone and rang the shipping company which owned the SS Vaxholm. She quickly found out that an English football team were on the Vaxholm. The team was called Millham United, and came from London. Millham United were in Sweden as part of a tour of Scandinavia. They were on the SS Vaxholm for a sightseeing trip around Stockholm's many islands. Monika made another phone call.

'Strand Hotel. Can I help you?'

'Yes. My name's Monika Lundgren. I'm a journalist on the newspaper *Dagens Nyheter*. I believe the Millham United team are staying at the Strand.'

'Yes. That is, they *were* staying here. But they've just left. They're on their way to Finland.'

'Do you know how they're travelling?' Monika asked.

'By ferry. On the Mariella.'

Chapter 3 *On the Mariella*

Monika knocked on Blom's door and went into his office.

'I'm happy that Carlsson is OK,' she began. 'But I should have seen the danger.'

'There was nothing you could do,' Blom said in his low voice. 'Tell me what you did see.'

She told Blom about the light from the boat, the metal noise and that she didn't hear the noise of a gun.

'And do we know who was on the SS Vaxholm?' Blom asked.

'An English football team called Millham United.'

'Interesting!' Blom said slowly. 'I've just sent a fax to MI5 in London. I think right-wing terrorists in Britain and Sweden might be working together. Perhaps these terrorists have something to do with the shooting of Carlsson. Where are the football team staying?'

'They were staying at the Strand Hotel,' Monika replied. 'But now they're going to Finland.'

'How are they travelling?' Blom asked.

'They're leaving this evening by ferry, the Mariella,' Monika replied.

'Take the ferry with them,' Blom said. 'Watch them, and find out all you can. You can be back in Stockholm by tomorrow night.'

Monika left the SMI offices and walked quickly through the crowds towards Stadsgården and the ferry to Finland.

The Mariella was a huge white and red ship. It was as big as a city building. Monika bought a ticket to Helsinki, and went on to the ferry. She watched cars and lorries drive on to the ferry. There were quite a few coaches as well. Monika smiled when she saw a coach with a sign saying 'Millham United'.

An hour later the Mariella moved slowly away from Stadsgården and out into Stockholm's archipelago. It would take two hours to move slowly through the hundreds of small islands of the archipelago before reaching the sea. Then it would cross to Helsinki during the night while everyone slept. Monika enjoyed travelling by ship. It was relaxing.

Monika looked down as the Mariella passed close to a small island with a red and white house on it. The house seemed so small next to the huge ship. Two small blonde-haired children ran out of the house. The children waved their hands at the ship. Monika waved back to the children. The Mariella passed sailing boats with yellow and blue Swedish flags, and a larger white passenger boat like the SS Vaxholm.

She thought about who had shot Carlsson. Why? Why hadn't she heard a gun? What was the sudden, bright light on the SS Vaxholm? How can you shoot someone without a gun?

Monika went inside and had a meal. The restaurant was full of passengers, but she couldn't see any who looked like English footballers.

The ship's nightclub was open. Monika went in and sat on her own. A waiter brought her a drink. The nightclub was quite dark and a band was playing on a platform in one corner. Some people were dancing, men and women together and women in groups of women.

A group of young men stood by the bar with glasses in their hands. They were laughing and talking. Now and then they watched the women dancing. They looked like sportsmen. Monika couldn't hear what language they were speaking. But their clothes didn't look Swedish. She was sure they were the Millham United team.

The band stopped to have a twenty-minute break.

'Does anyone want to play?' the guitarist asked as the band left the room.

One of the men at the bar shouted 'Yes, me!' He walked over from the bar to the guitarist.

He was a tall man with long red hair. He sat down and picked up the guitar. He was very good. He played fast rock music, and then slow love songs. Monika watched him. She couldn't help watching. She loved music. She let the music fill her.

The guitarist saw Monika watching him. He smiled at her. She smiled back.

When the band came back the red-haired man returned the guitar. He smiled, and then walked over to Monika.

'Hi,' the man said in English. 'I'm Bruce.'

'You play wonderfully,' Monika said.

'Thank you,' Bruce replied with a smile. 'Do you want to dance?'

Monika thought 'Why not?' She smiled and got up.

Bruce and Monika danced for half an hour. Bruce danced as well as he played the guitar.

'Are you on holiday?' she asked.

'Yes,' Bruce replied. 'I'm travelling with Millham

United. I go everywhere to see them play. Do you like football?'

'Yes,' Monika lied.

'And are you on holiday?' Bruce continued.

'Yes,' Monika lied again. 'I'm going to visit some friends in Helsinki.'

After they had danced Bruce introduced Monika to some of the players in the football team. They all seemed very friendly. She asked questions and learnt a lot about Millham United. They had finished their visit to Sweden and were now going to play one game in Helsinki. Then they would go back to London by coach and ferry. But they were coming back to Stockholm for a match in two weeks' time.

'Do you always travel by coach?' Monika asked one of the players.

'Yes,' he said, 'always. Although we did fly when we went to South Africa.'

Bruce asked Monika to dance again, but she said she had to get up early. Then she left the nightclub, went to her room and locked the door.

'Millham United seem OK,' she thought. It was strange, though, that they always travelled by coach.

Chapter 4   *Leave her alone!*

The Mariella moved slowly into Helsinki. It was morning. Monika watched the city get closer. Soon she could see the roofs of houses, a church and tall buildings.

Suddenly she heard a voice she knew.

'Here! It's her! She's the one who pushed me in the water!'

It was the English football fan. It was the young man who she had pushed into the water outside the City Hall. His face was even redder. He looked very angry. And he wasn't alone. Six other young men with shaved heads and big boots were with him.

The English fans started singing.

'Here we go! Here we go!' they sang as they quickly made a circle around Monika. The circle closed around her.

'Get her!' one of the fans shouted.

Monika looked at the circle of red, smiling faces. They were like animals. The leader was the fan who she had pushed in the water. He came closer to her.

'Stop!' Monika heard someone shout. 'Stop it now!'

It was Bruce. The football fans turned to look at him.

'Do what I say,' Bruce said. 'Leave her alone! Go and get on the bus!'

Then a strange thing happened. The young men did what Bruce told them. They went away.

'Thank you,' Monika said. 'I don't know what to say.'

'That's all right,' Bruce said. 'I'm sorry. Some of these fans don't know when to stop.'

'But they did stop! They did what you told them!' Monika said in surprise.

'Yes,' Bruce said. 'I know them quite well. We travel together a lot.'

'I see,' Monika said slowly. 'I didn't realise they were your friends.'

Bruce smiled. 'We're all Millham fans,' he said. 'It's lucky we met now. I wanted to see you again. I'm not doing anything today. Would you like to have lunch and a look around Helsinki?'

'No, I'm sorry,' she said. 'I can't. I've got to go back to Stockholm.' She really was sorry and she suddenly felt lonely. She would like to spend the day with him. But she was working.

'But I thought you were on holiday,' Bruce said quickly.

Monika shook her head. 'I can't explain,' she said.

'Your phone number,' Bruce continued. 'Give me your phone number in Stockholm.'

'No, I'm sorry,' Monika replied. 'I have to go now.'

She turned and walked away from Bruce. The Mariella was in Helsinki now and Monika left the ship. Two hours later she was on a plane back to Stockholm.

*   *   *

'MI5 are sending a man called Chapman over this evening on the late British Airways flight,' Blom said to Monika. They were in his office. 'Chapman's going to help us. Can you go and meet him at the airport?'

'And what about the Millham United team?' Monika asked.

'We'll ask the police in Finland to watch them,' replied Blom. 'And there's something else you should know. We still don't know how Carlsson was shot. The police haven't found a bullet.'

*   *   *

James Chapman was a tall, slim Englishman of about thirty. He had a small moustache, black hair and blue eyes. He was wearing an expensive suit and had a small bag over his shoulder.

'Oh,' Chapman said in a cold voice when Monika introduced herself. 'So you're Lundgren. I was expecting a man, not a girl.'

'I'm not a girl,' Monica replied gently, 'I'm a woman.'

Chapman then refused to go into Stockholm by bus. He wanted to go by taxi.

'But taxis are very expensive,' Monika explained.

'Never mind,' replied Chapman. In the taxi Chapman talked about himself, and how good a secret agent he was. He didn't seem interested in the Carlsson shooting. He told her about all the countries he had visited.

'I've never been to Sweden before,' he said. 'I expect it's an interesting little place.'

Monika looked angrily at him.

'Sweden is not a little place,' she said. 'It's much bigger than England!'

'Oh, I say,' said Chapman. 'Now, now, don't get angry.'

'Let's talk about the shooting of Carlsson,' Monika replied.

Chapman listened, and said nothing as Monika told him what had happened. By the time Monika had finished, the taxi had arrived at the Strand Hotel where Chapman was staying.

'Now, my dear,' Chapman said, taking Monika's arm. 'Let's go somewhere nice and have dinner.'

'I'm terribly sorry,' she said. 'I'm afraid I can't join you. I'll call at the hotel for you at eight o'clock tomorrow morning.' She was pleased to leave Chapman. She thought he was boring and rude.

The next morning Monika took Chapman to the City Hall to see the place where Carlsson was shot. The police were still there. Divers were working underwater to try and find the bullet.

'I'd like to dive underwater,' Chapman said.

'OK,' Monika said. 'Me too.' She had become an expert diver in the USA.

They put on wet suits in the City Hall and then they dived for an hour. They found nothing. They dived again in the afternoon. Nothing. At four o'clock the police were ready to stop. Chapman had started to take off his wet suit.

'Once more,' Monika said. 'There must be something in the water.'

Monika worked carefully in the dark water. Then she felt something under her fingers on the bottom. She picked it up and swam up to the top. She looked at what she had found. It was a small piece of metal, like the top of a pen.

'What do you think it is?' Monika asked.

'I don't know,' said Chapman. 'I'm sure it's nothing. Throw it away.'

'No,' Monika replied. 'I think I'll show it to Blom.' They took off their wet suits, and went back to the SMI offices.

Monika walked in and put the piece of metal on Blom's desk. 'What's this?' she asked.

Blom picked up the piece of metal and looked at it. 'It's a crossbow bolt,' he replied. 'Now, a crossbow looks like this,' and he drew a picture.

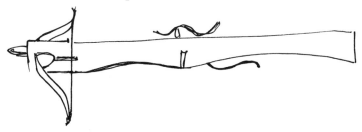

'It's an old weapon that people used to use hundreds of years ago. It's not heavy and it's very strong. It shoots a heavy piece of metal called a bolt. A crossbow bolt can kill someone over a hundred metres away.'

'That's why I didn't hear a shot,' said Monika. 'And perhaps the noise I heard was the bolt. The bolt went right through Carlsson. It hit the ground and fell into the water.'

Blom looked up at Monika. 'Yes, I think you're right,' he said. 'And perhaps the bolt came from the SS Vaxholm.'

'But what was the light I saw on the SS Vaxholm?' Monika asked.

'I don't know yet,' Blom answered. 'But we'll find out.'

Chapman said nothing, then coughed. 'Excuse me,' he said. 'If you don't need me, I think I'll go back to the hotel.'

'Fine,' Blom said. 'See you tomorrow.'

'Bye,' Monika said. She watched Chapman leave the room. After he had gone she turned to Blom.

'He's not much help,' she said.

Chapter 5 *I want you to go to London*

The next day, Blom, Monika and Chapman met in Blom's office.

Blom was talking about a terrorist group in Sweden called 'Nordlandet'.

'Basically,' he said, ' "Nordlandet" believe that white people should rule the world. They are a small group. They are not very strong. Few people agree with them.'

'We have similar groups in Britain,' Chapman replied. He started to talk about terrorism, but was soon talking about himself. He talked for forty minutes. Blom and Monika learnt a lot about how clever Chapman was, and very little about terrorists.

'Excuse me,' Blom said. 'Can I ask a question? Is it possible that terrorists use football clubs to hide their activities?'

Chapman laughed. 'What a strange question!' he said. 'No, I don't think so. But anything is possible.'

Chapman stayed in Stockholm for two more days. Blom and Monika showed him what they knew about 'Nordlandet' and other groups. Chapman talked and talked, but said very little. Each night he asked Monika to have dinner with him, and each night she refused.

Then it was Friday and time for Chapman to return to London. He said goodbye to Blom and Monika at the SMI offices.

'Would you like me to come to the airport with you?' Monika asked politely.

'Thank you,' Chapman replied. 'But it's not necessary. I've enjoyed my visit to your little country – and I've learnt a lot! I hope you find the person who shot Carlsson. And from what I've seen, I'd forget about all these terrorist groups if I were you. Cheerio!' he said and left.

'Do you think he's right?' Monika asked. 'A terrorist group didn't try and kill Carlsson?'

'I don't know, but I want you to go to London this afternoon. I want you to find out more about this football team,' Blom said.

Monika nodded. 'Shall I tell Chapman I'm coming to London?' she asked.

'Not immediately,' Blom said. 'In my opinion he talks a lot and does very little. MI5 were probably happy to send him away. Now they can have him back. No, go to London and see what you can find out yourself.'

Chapter 6 *Monika couldn't believe her eyes!*

Monika took the early afternoon SAS flight to London and checked into the Scandic Crown Hotel, near Victoria Station. She had a map of London, and knew where Millham United's stadium was.

She decided to go there first.

She left the hotel at eight o'clock in the evening and took a taxi to the Millham United stadium in East London. There were lots of people near the stadium and the lights were on.

'Is there a match tonight?' Monika asked the taxi driver.

'No,' the taxi driver replied. 'There's a concert.'

Then Monika saw a large sign.

WHITE ROCK CONCERT

Monika paid and went in. There were about two thousand people in the stadium. Most were men and most had shaved heads and big boots. There was a platform in the middle of the stadium.

The lights went on. A tall, red-haired man carrying a guitar walked on to the front of the platform. Everyone shouted. Then the red-haired man began to play.

Monika watched in great surprise. It was Bruce, the man she had met on the Mariella.

Bruce started to play. He was brilliant – even better than on the Mariella. Monika listened and watched for half an hour, forgetting where she was. She liked this man. 'Maybe when this is over,' she thought, 'we can go out together.'

Then she remembered why she was at Millham United stadium and left the concert.

The rest of the football stadium was dark. Outside there was a car park, and some lights were on here. Monika found a door. It was open so she went in. Inside she saw changing rooms, showers and football things. There was no-one there.

She went on to an area of offices. There were lots of doors, but they were all locked. Everything was dark. Then she saw a light coming from under a door. Monika walked quietly up to the door. She could hear voices. Monika listened carefully. There were several men talking. It was hard to hear what they were saying. They were speaking English, but Monika was sure at least one of the men was foreign. 'Perhaps Swedish,' she thought.

Monika heard people moving in the room. Someone was coming to the door! There was nowhere to hide. If she ran away they would see her. The sound of someone walking towards the door became clearer. Monika turned. There was another door opposite and she ran over to it. The door wasn't locked. She opened it and felt fresh air on her face. She was out in the car park.

She quickly closed the door and looked around. She saw some cars and a coach. The only light came from a high window. It was the room where the men were. Monika climbed on to one of the cars. Then she jumped from the car roof to the coach. The coach was next to the window. Moving carefully she went across the roof to the office window.

It was easy to see into the office from the coach roof. There were four men and one woman in the room. One man was sitting at a table. He was aged about fifty, and had lots of black hair. Sitting next to him was a tall man in sports clothes and trainers. He looked about thirty.

Standing near the desk were three people. The woman was in her early twenties. She had short blonde hair and was wearing jeans and a black jacket. Next to her was a man of the same age with a shaved head, also in jeans and a black jacket. He had his hand on the woman's shoulder. The couple in black jackets were laughing.

They were laughing at something the fifth person was saying. He was much older, at least sixty. He had white hair, a white beard, a dark sun-tan, and was very fat.

'Damn!' Monika said to herself. 'Now I can see them but I can't hear them! I'm sure the couple in black jackets are Swedish. But who are the others?'

She watched and waited. The white-haired man and the young couple sat down at the table. The white-haired man took some papers and a map out of a bag. He talked to the others and pointed at the map.

'I wish I could hear what he is saying,' Monika thought. 'And what country does the map show?'

Suddenly the man in sports clothes stood up. The others looked at him.

'He's seen me,' Monika thought.

But the man hadn't seen Monika. He walked over to the door and opened it. Another man walked into the room. He went up to the table and shook hands with everyone. Then he started talking quickly. The others listened carefully.

Monika couldn't believe her eyes. She knew the man who had just come into the room. It was Chapman!

Monika felt in her jeans pocket. She carefully took out a very small camera which looked like a cigarette lighter. Monika photographed the people in the room through the window. No-one saw her on the coach roof. No-one heard her jump down from the coach and run across the car park. No-one saw her climb the car park wall, and get out into the street outside the football stadium.

A taxi passed and Monika stopped it. 'The Scandic Crown Hotel, please. Near Victoria Station.'

The next morning Monika got up early, and took the 7.15 SAS flight back to Stockholm. By one o'clock she was at the SMI offices. By two o'clock her photographs were ready. Monika looked at the photos carefully, and then made some phone calls. Then she took the photos with her to Blom's office. She told Blom about her evening at Millham United's stadium and showed him the photos.

'I know who the two men at the table are now,' Monika said. 'I've just spoken to a football reporter on *Dagens Nyheter*. They are Harry Dixon, Chairman of Millham United, and Danny Worthington, the club's manager. And of course you recognise Chapman. But I don't know who the others are.'

Blom studied the photos for a minute. Then he looked up. 'I'm pretty sure that the young man and woman are Kent Nyström and Gunilla Lippich – both from Gothenburg and both members of a right-wing group. We'll have to check.'

'But what was Chapman doing there?' Monika asked.

'Perhaps he was finding out about the football team,'

Blom said slowly. 'Perhaps he's changed his mind about terrorists and football clubs.'

'But he was telling them something,' Monika replied. 'He wasn't listening.'

'Let's find out who the older man is,' Blom said. 'Then we'll decide what to do.'

Monika left Blom's office and went to the SMI information centre. She put a description of the white-haired man into a computer and waited. A minute later there was a list of names on the screen – it was a long list. Monika printed out the list and studied it. Then she went back to the computer and started work. She put in the names one by one and pictures appeared on the screen. The list of over two hundred names was in alphabetical order. It wasn't until she got to the letter 'V' that Monika had some luck.

'That's him, I'm sure,' she thought. She printed out the picture and some details and ran to Blom's office.

'The old man is Adolf Vitjord,' Monika shouted excitedly. 'He's the leader of a South African right-wing party, now thought to be living part of the time in Mozambique.'

'Well done!' Blom replied with a big smile. 'Now why were the football team manager and chairman meeting two young Swedes and a South African? And what has it got to do with the shooting of Carlsson?'

'And what was Chapman doing there?' Monika added.

'Let's ask Chapman himself,' Blom said and picked up the phone. 'Get me MI5 in London,' he said quietly. 'I want to speak to Mr Chapman.'

Chapter 7 *Here's something for you*

'Is that Chapman?' Blom asked. 'Blom here. Listen, there's something I want to tell you and a question I want to ask you.'

Monika watched Blom's face as he talked to Chapman. Blom told him about Monika's visit to Millham United, and the meeting she had seen. But he didn't say that she had taken photographs. He also didn't say that they knew who the people at the meeting were.

Then Blom said, 'And my question is: what were you doing there?' Blom was silent and listened. From time to time he nodded and said, 'Yes, I see.'

Then Blom said, 'No, she couldn't hear what the people in the room were saying. And no . . .' Blom raised his voice and sat forward in his wheelchair, '. . . she wasn't spying on you. How could she know you would be there?'

Blom was silent again, then said thank you and put the phone down. He sat silently for a moment and thought. Then he looked at Monika.

'Well,' Blom said, 'our friend Mr Chapman says he went to Millham United's stadium to help us. He was trying to find out about the football club for us. He says that he was at the meeting to ask questions. He says the other people at the meeting were football fans. They were discussing the team's next visit to Sweden. He's very angry that we didn't tell him you were in London,' Blom continued. 'He thinks you were spying on him.'

'Do you believe him?' Monika asked.

'I don't know. Maybe it's just a misunderstanding,' said Blom.

'Did he have any new information?'

'No.'

'So what do we do now?' asked Monika.

'I want you to go to South Africa. We need to know more about Vitjord.'

Monika looked at Blom in surprise. 'But he's in London,' she said.

'Vitjord was in London yesterday,' Blom said. 'But he'll return to South Africa. Go and wait for him. Try and find out why he's so interested in Millham United football team. Talk to him if you can.'

'But I can't say I'm from the SMI,' Monika said.

Blom smiled. 'I'm sure you'll think of something to say,' he said. 'Now you'd better go and pack some clothes. Be back here at five. We'll book you on a plane to South Africa tonight.'

Monika left the SMI offices and walked back to her flat. Half of her felt great: Blom trusted her and she was going on an important trip. The other half wasn't so sure: she had never been to South Africa and she hadn't liked what she had seen of Vitjord. 'And what has all this got to do with the shooting of Carlsson?' she asked herself.

An hour later Monika was back in Blom's office.

'You're booked on this evening's SAS flight to Johannesburg from Copenhagen,' Blom said with a quick smile. 'Your flight to Copenhagen leaves in two hours. We haven't got much time. Here's a copy of the fax booking your hotel – you're staying at the Carlton Hotel in the centre of Johannesburg. Stay there until you hear from me. One of our agents, Joseph, works at the hotel. He will help you if necessary, and will also give you my messages. OK?'

'Yes,' Monika replied.

'Very well, then,' Blom said, and took two small bags from his jacket pocket. 'Here's something for you.'

'What are they?' Monika asked.

'Presents,' Blom replied with a laugh.

Monika opened the first bag. It felt hard. It was a Walkman – quite an expensive one.

'Well,' Monika said. 'Thank you!'

The second bag was softer and Monika opened it carefully. It felt like something to wear. Monika took the present out. It was a blue bikini. Monika looked at the bikini in surprise. She laughed.

Blom took the bikini from her and held up the top half.

'Do you see this?' he asked.

'Yes,' replied Monika. 'It's a bikini top.'

'Yes, but it is also a radio,' said Blom. 'There are very small wires in the top which catch sounds. The sounds are sent to the Walkman. When you wear the bikini and listen to the Walkman you can hear people's conversations from twenty metres away.'

'Well,' Monika said, 'of course I'll take it, but I'm going to work, not lie on the beach!'

'Take it with you anyway,' Blom said. 'We know Vitjord stays at the Carlton Hotel sometimes. And there is a swimming pool at the hotel.'

'All right,' she said and put the Walkman and bikini in her bag. She looked at her watch. 'I must go.'

Chapter 8   *Who's the girl?*

Monika felt a push in her back as the giant plane started to move, slowly at first, then quicker and quicker. Suddenly the nose of the plane lifted and the SAS 747 took off for Johannesburg. She looked out onto the wing and remembered the woman standing on the wing of the Boeing Stearman plane at the Water Festival. She wondered if it really was a dangerous thing to do, and then she wondered how dangerous Vitjord was.

Ten hours later the 747 was over Johannesburg. Monika looked down at the city. She could see tall modern buildings, large areas of low, poor houses on the edge of the city, and huge piles of earth from the gold mines.

The Carlton Hotel was big and expensive. A smartly-dressed hotel porter opened Monika's taxi door. Another porter carried her suitcase into the hotel. Monika checked in and found there was a note for her.

Have a rest. I will get in touch with you soon. Blom.

She went to her room, had a shower and slept. It was early evening when she woke. She got dressed and went for a walk outside the hotel, but didn't go far. She passed lines of people waiting for minibuses. The women wore coloured woollen hats and scarves. A barber was shaving a man's head by the side of the road. Monika was the only white person walking and people looked at her. A police car stopped and asked if she wanted help. Monika said no, but walked quickly back to the hotel.

The next morning she found the swimming pool on the roof of the hotel.

There was no-one else by the swimming pool. The area around the pool had glass sides and Monika could look down at the city. Her hotel was full of rich business people and tourists, most of them white. The streets outside were a mixture of rich and poor; most of the poor people were black.

Monika lay by the pool and thought about her work. 'There are lots of questions. Why did someone shoot Carlsson? What was Vitjord doing in London? What about Millham United? And what about Chapman? What was he doing?'

On the second day nothing happened. Monika ate alone in the evening in a restaurant next to the hotel. She began to wonder what she was doing there.

On the third day, as she was going up in the lift to the swimming pool one of the hotel porters got in the lift with her, and gave her a note. The note was from Blom.

'What's your name?' Monika asked.

'Joseph, madam,' the porter said. 'If there is anything I can do, let me know.'

Monika got out of the lift on the eighth floor and went to the pool. She read Blom's note.

Vitjord in Johannesburg. Meeting at Carlton today. Watch carefully.

Monika lay down by the pool, and listened to music on the Walkman. It was hot and she felt tired. Through windows of the pool she could see the town and the gold mines around Johannesburg. Monika fell asleep.

'Hi!' someone shouted.

Monika woke up. There were other people by the pool now. Three men were sitting at a table about ten metres away. Another man was walking towards them. He had white hair and a beard. It was Vitjord.

'Hi,' Vitjord said again to the three men. He sat down at the table and they started talking.

Monika put on her sunglasses and pulled her hat down over her head. Then she lay on her side, put a cassette into the Walkman and pressed RECORD. She could hear every word of the men's conversation.

Vitjord was telling the men about his visit to London. Monika listened in horror. She couldn't believe her ears. Vitjord was buying a nuclear weapon.

'We're getting the bomb this week,' he said. 'Our friends are picking it up in Russia and bringing it to London. Then my private plane will fly the bomb to Mozambique. From Mozambique we will bring the bomb here. When we've got it here, we can take over the South African government. We will have the power here, and make South Africa once again the greatest white country in the world!'

The other men smiled and nodded. Vitjord smiled back. Then his face became serious again.

'There's only one problem,' Vitjord continued, 'Carlsson. He is much better now. Governments and businesses have given a lot of money since he was shot. Soon Carlsson will have enough money. And then the Russians will be able to destroy their nuclear weapons. We must stop Carlsson. One bomb is not enough for us. We need lots of bombs.'

'Why didn't we kill Carlsson in Stockholm?' one of the men asked.

'There'll be another chance,' Vitjord replied. 'Carlsson's out of hospital now. It's Friday today. He's having another meeting in Stockholm next Friday. First we'll get our bomb and then we'll get Carlsson!' Vitjord hit the table with his hand.

Then one of the men looked around and saw Monika.

'Who's the girl?' he said. 'She keeps on looking at you.'

'I don't know,' replied Vitjord. ' Go and get her.'

Monika quickly got to her feet and walked over to the lift. She heard someone behind her. One of the men shouted. 'Hey, stop!'

Monika jumped into the lift and pressed Ground Floor. There was someone else in the lift. It was Joseph. She pulled the cassette out of the Walkman and gave it to Joseph.

'Send this to Blom, please,' she said.

The lift stopped at the third floor and Joseph got out. Monika continued to the ground floor.

The hotel entrance hall was busy. People looked at Monika in her bikini. She saw two men talking into radios. The men walked towards her. She tried to get back into the lift but the doors were closed. She waited. The lift doors opened and Monika stepped in.

'Hi!' a voice said. It was Vitjord. The lift doors closed.

Chapter 9   *Why were you looking at me?*

The smartly-dressed hotel porter closed the back door of the white Mercedes. The car was new, and had dark windows. The driver started the engine, and the car moved quietly and smoothly away from the Carlton Hotel.

Traffic was heavy in the city and the white car moved slowly. As the car left the city centre the traffic became much easier and the car went faster. It headed to the north of the city where rich people lived. The car passed tall green and purple trees and high walls with glass on the top. Behind the walls were large houses with swimming pools. A few people walked along the side of the road. But these people didn't live in that area. They were the people who worked in the large houses; the people who did the cooking and cleaning.

Monika sat in the back seat of the Mercedes with Vitjord. She was his guest. He was taking her to his house for lunch. When the lift doors had closed in the Carlton Monika had thought quickly.

'Why were you looking at me?' Vitjord had asked.

'Because I've always wanted to meet you,' Monika had replied. She had told Vitjord that she was on holiday in South Africa, and that she was Swedish. She had said that some of her friends, Kent and Gunilla, had told her about him, and that she thought he was wonderful.

'And what's your name?' Vitjord had asked.

'Maria,' Monika had replied. 'Maria Svenson.'

'Well, Maria,' Vitjord had said, taking Monika's arm and smiling. 'Would you like to have lunch with me?'

Monika had agreed. She had gone to her room and changed. In her jeans pocket she had put her wallet and her passport. Then she had joined Vitjord outside the hotel.

As she sat in the back of the Mercedes Monika thought to herself, 'What am I doing here? In the back of a car with the man who tried to kill Carlsson. I must be mad!'

The Mercedes slowed down, turned, and then stopped outside tall wooden doors. The doors were in a tall, yellow wall and there was broken glass on top of the wall. The Mercedes drove in up to a large, yellow house which was set in a beautiful garden. There was a big swimming pool, and a black gardener was watering the grass.

Monika went into the house with Vitjord. They sat in a beautiful room which had lots of photographs on the walls. Vitjord offered Monika a drink.

'An orange juice, please,' she replied.

'Nothing stronger?' Vitjord asked, and gave himself a large drink.

Monika didn't know what would happen next. She was afraid Vitjord would ask her lots of questions. She needn't have worried. Vitjord was happy to talk about himself. He told Monika how he hated black people. He explained that he now lived in Mozambique for part of the year. He had his own army there. One day he would return to South Africa with his army and take over. He told her that soon the whole world would know who he was. Soon he would be one of the most important men in the world. Monika listened and said nothing. She was afraid. Vitjord was mad. Completely mad. And he was buying a nuclear weapon!

Her mother had been right. She should have gone to university and not joined the army!

A telephone rang in another room.

'Excuse me,' Vitjord said and got up. 'Help yourself to another drink.' He left the room.

Monika got up. But she didn't get herself a drink. She walked around the room looking at the photographs. They were all pictures of Vitjord. Vitjord dressed as a soldier. Vitjord talking to a crowd. Vitjord with guns. Vitjord standing by what looked like dead bodies.

'You like my pictures, yes?'

Monika jumped. Vitjord was standing right behind her. Although he was a big man he moved very quietly.

Monika nodded. 'Where's that?' she asked pointing to the picture with the bodies.

'Namibia,' Vitjord replied. 'We killed lots of blacks there.'

Monika felt sick. What was she doing here? she thought again.

Vitjord was still standing behind Monika. Suddenly she felt his arms around her. He held her strongly so she couldn't move.

'Just a moment,' Monika said, with a weak laugh. 'Where's the toilet? I've just got to go to the toilet.'

Vitjord laughed loudly and let her go. 'It's near the front door. Don't be long,' he said. 'I'll be waiting.'

She walked quickly to the toilet and opened the door. But she didn't go into the toilet. She closed the toilet door loudly and walked out of the front door. She suddenly felt the hot air on her face. She looked around the garden and saw that the gardener was still watering. The Mercedes was there. And the keys were inside!

Monika jumped into the Mercedes and started the engine. There was a shout! It was the gardener. Another shout! The driver was running out of the house. Monika turned the car quickly on the wet grass. She looked in the mirror and saw Vitjord at the front door. He had a gun.

There was a loud bang! Vitjord was shooting at her! Monika drove the Mercedes straight at the wooden doors. The engine screamed. The doors broke, and the Mercedes drove through into the street.

Vitjord ran out into the street behind the Mercedes and shot several times. He hit the car twice, but didn't hurt Monika. She had escaped! Then she started thinking. How was she going to get out of South Africa? She couldn't go back to the hotel. Luckily she had her passport with her. And Vitjord was looking for a blonde called Maria Svenson.

Monika slowed down when she had driven a few kilometres away from Vitjord's house. She didn't want to be stopped by the police. She drove slowly, and soon found what she was looking for: a shopping centre.

She bought a red dress, red shoes, a large white hat and dark glasses. She also bought a bottle of black hair colour and went into the nearest toilet. Twenty minutes later she came out with black hair, wearing the new clothes.

She then drove the Mercedes to Jan Smuts Airport. It was two o'clock. As she walked into the building she was stopped by a white policeman. Monika's heart jumped.

'Yes?' she said.

'Any guns?' the policeman asked and searched her. 'Thank you. Have a nice day.'

Monika smiled to herself. Now all she had to do was buy

a ticket. She looked at the TV screen with flight information.

'Oh no!' The first flight to Europe was not until eight in the evening. She couldn't wait until then.

Then Monika saw a face she knew. It was one of Vitjord's friends from the Carlton. He walked past her without stopping. The disguise was working!

Monika knew she couldn't stay at the airport all day. Where was the next flight going to? She looked at the flight information. Maputo in Mozambique. Great. She'd always wanted to go to Mozambique.

The LAM Mozambican Airways flight to Maputo left half an hour later.

The flight to Maputo was quite short. Monika thought about washing her hair in the toilet, but there was no water. She sat back in her seat and thought about Vitjord and his plans. She hoped that Joseph had sent the cassette to Blom. When she got to Maputo she would try and get another flight to Stockholm as soon as possible.

'I wonder what my parents would say if they could see me now,' she thought.

Then she heard a voice that she knew. It was one of Vitjord's friends from the Carlton – the one she had seen at the airport. He was sitting right in front of her! There was another man beside him.

'I wonder where that Swedish woman is – the one who stole Vitjord's car,' the voice said. 'She wasn't at the airport, and she isn't on this plane. I've looked and there aren't any blonde women.'

'Well,' the other man replied. 'I wouldn't like to be her when Vitjord catches her.' They both laughed.

Chapter 10 *Can I help you?*

The LAM 737 turned and began to lose height as it got closer to Maputo, the capital of Mozambique. Monika could see the silver Indian Ocean with a few small fishing boats and a large ship near the coast. The land was flat and brown, with a few small trees here and there.

The airport came closer, and Monika could see its name MAPUTO in white stones on the grass. The 737 turned and came in to land. She was on the wing of the plane again, she thought. Living dangerously. The plane landed and stopped outside a small green airport building. The passengers got off the plane and walked to the building.

There was a sign saying 'Passports'. Vitjord's friends from the Carlton were right behind Monika as she went into the airport building. Monika showed her passport to the Mozambican passport officer.

'Excuse me,' he said. 'What is your name?'

'Monika Lundgren,' Monika replied with another smile.

'But this isn't you,' the passport officer said. He held the passport in his hand and showed Monika the photograph in the passport. Then she felt someone pushing her from behind. It was one of the men from the plane, one of Vitjord's men. He was looking at her photo in the passport.

'I'm sorry, this isn't your photo,' the Mozambican passport officer said to Monika. 'Please come this way.'

Monika followed the passport officer into a small office.

She was happy to be there. Anywhere rather than next to Vitjord's men. Monika sat and waited alone. It was hot in the office and the window was open.

'I'm sorry to keep you waiting,' a voice said. The speaker was a short man with a smiling, round face and a beard. 'My name's Cabinda,' he said. 'Passport police.'

'I can explain,' Monika said quickly. 'My hair. It's not like the photograph. I know. I bought hair colour in South Africa. I can wash it and show you.'

Cabinda looked carefully at Monika and then at the photo. 'No, that's OK. I can see that it's you,' Cabinda said. 'There's one more thing. You need a visa. It's ten dollars. You can pay the passport officer. Welcome to Mozambique!'

Monika paid for her visa and, as she didn't have a suitcase, walked straight out into the warm air.

There were a few people waiting outside the airport building, but the bus to Maputo had gone. The air was warm and Monika felt happy. Other people were walking into Maputo and she decided to walk too.

As she was walking a van slowed and stopped beside her. It was a big white van with black windows. The van stopped in front of her. Two men got out. They were Vitjord's men. One of them opened the van's back doors.

'Get in,' the bearded man said and tried to take her arm. Monika pulled away from him. Some people stopped to look. No-one said anything. Then Monika heard another engine, and then a friendly voice.

'Can I help you?' the voice said. Monika turned around. It was Cabinda from the passport police. He was getting out of an old yellow lorry which was full of people.

Monika smiled. 'Yes, please,' she replied.

'Can I help you?' Cabinda asked the men.

The men stood for a minute and looked at him, then they got back into the white van. The bearded man looked out of the black window and spoke to Monika.

'We'll find you,' he said. 'Maputo's a small town.'

The white van drove off towards the city centre.

'Do you know those men?' Cabinda asked.

'No,' Monika replied. 'Not really. Thank you very much for your help.'

Cabinda smiled. 'It's nothing,' he said. 'But it's quite a long way to the city centre. Where are you staying?'

'I don't know,' Monika said.

'Well,' Cabinda said in his friendly voice. 'We'll find you somewhere. But first we must get to the centre.'

Cabinda pointed to the lorry. 'We call this a "chapa",' he said. 'Come with us.'

Monika looked at the chapa. It was old and there seemed to be at least fifty people standing in the back.

'OK,' she replied. 'Thank you very much.'

The chapa drove slowly into Maputo. There were more and more people walking along the road. The air was hot and dry. There were small houses made from wood beside the road. Children were playing outside them. Slowly the wooden houses became bigger, and then became large buildings.

Monika held on to Cabinda's arm as the chapa hit a hole in the road. The chapa stopped from time to time and people got on and off.

'What's that?' Monika asked as they passed a very tall half-finished building.

Cabinda smiled and then replied. He had to shout because of the noise of the chapa. 'It's a present from the Portuguese,' he said. 'When the Portuguese left my country in 1975 they took everything they could with them. And they destroyed everything they couldn't take. That building was going to be a hotel. But as they left the Portuguese filled the inside with concrete. Now it's no use to anyone.'

The chapa was soon near the centre of Maputo.

'Let's get off here,' Cabinda said. 'And we'll find you somewhere to stay.' He helped Monika down from the high lorry.

'I need to find a hotel,' Monika said. 'And make a phone call. And find the Swedish Embassy. But I'm sure I can look after myself.'

'Don't be silly,' Cabinda replied. 'You are a guest in our country. I would invite you to stay in my apartment, but it's very small and I have a very large family!' He laughed.

The first hotels Cabinda and Monika tried were all full. Finally, they found a room at the Polana Hotel, a little way out of the centre of town.

'Thank you very much for all your help,' Monika said. 'I don't know what to say.'

'Then say nothing,' Cabinda replied. 'Tonight my wife and I will take you out to dinner at the Feira Popular. There are a lot of good restaurants there. Be ready – we'll come for you at eight o'clock!'

With a smile and a wave Cabinda left the Polana, and Monika was shown to her room. It was a very pleasant hotel with a view of some yellow palm trees and the deep blue Indian Ocean.

Monika wanted to call SMI. The hotel though, wasn't safe. She would have to find the Swedish Embassy.

The Swedish Embassy was close to the Polana on Avenida Julius Nyerere. Christer Sandelin was the Swedish Consul. He was tall and thin with a blonde beard. He was a nice man and after making a few phone calls to check Monika's identity he rang Anders Blom.

'What are you doing in Mozambique?' asked Blom.

Monika explained and then asked, 'Have you received a cassette from me? I gave it to Joseph this morning at the Carlton.'

'No,' Blom replied. 'Not yet! Joseph will send it with the plane tonight and I will get it tomorrow morning.'

'Vitjord tried to kill Carlsson once and is going to try again,' Monika said. 'I think he knows who I am. He tried to kill me.'

'I want you back in Stockholm as soon as possible,' Blom replied. 'And stay in the hotel. Don't go out. I don't want Vitjord's men to catch you!'

'OK,' Monika said. 'I promise I'll stay in the hotel, and I'll let you know when I've got a plane ticket.'

They said goodbye. Monika thanked Christer and left the embassy. She walked slowly back to the hotel, enjoying the soft early evening air.

When she got back she washed the black hair colour out of her hair. Then she remembered that she was having dinner with Cabinda and his wife.

Chapter 11 *Now we've got you!*

At ten past eight the telephone in Monika's room rang.

'We're waiting for you at reception,' Cabinda said.

Monika opened her mouth to say that she was not going out. Then she changed her mind. It was just like Blom, talking to her like a child and telling her to stay in the hotel.

'I'm coming,' Monika said.

Cabinda and his wife Amelia were waiting in reception.

'Hello,' Cabinda said. 'Everything OK? You look like your passport photo now.' They both smiled.

'The Feira Popular,' Cabinda explained, 'is a fun fair with lots of good restaurants.'

Cabinda's wife, Amelia, spoke good English and Monika soon felt comfortable with them. At the fair they looked at several restaurants, and then chose one that served seafood. The restaurant wasn't full and they were able to talk easily. 'People here usually eat quite late,' Cabinda said. 'It's always full at midnight!'

Monika enjoyed being with Cabinda and Amelia. They told her about life in Mozambique, its joys and problems. Monika felt very much at ease with them. Then Cabinda asked, 'And what do you do for a living? Are you here on holiday? So far from Sweden and without a suitcase!'

Cabinda had helped her and Monika felt she should explain.

She didn't tell Cabinda and Amelia who she worked for, but she did tell them about Vitjord and the men at the airport. Cabinda listened carefully and nodded.

'This man Vitjord is well-known here,' Cabinda said when Monika had finished. 'Mozambique is a very big country, and Vitjord lives in an empty area near South Africa. People say he has his own army there. Our country is at peace now. But men like Vitjord are still very dangerous here. You must be careful while you are in Maputo.'

Monika told Amelia and Cabinda that she had to return to Stockholm at once.

'Oh dear,' Amelia said. 'Mozambique is beautiful. You must come again and stay longer.'

'There are direct flights from Maputo to Portugal and France,' Cabinda said. 'There's an Air France flight on Sunday to Paris.'

'I'll try and get a seat on that tomorrow,' Monika said. 'Now let me pay for this lovely meal.'

'Certainly not,' Cabinda said with a wide smile. 'While you are here you are our guest.'

Monika tried to make him change his mind, but it was impossible. Cabinda got up and went to pay. Amelia left the table to go to the toilet. Monika sat on her own.

'What kind, friendly people,' she thought.

'Hello, miss,' a voice said. Monika knew the voice. She looked up. Vitjord's friends were standing by her table.

'We said we'd find you,' the man with the beard said.

Monika looked around. She couldn't see Cabinda or Amelia. Behind the two men she could see their white van.

The bearded man took Monika's arm. 'Come for a ride

with us,' he said with a nasty smile and pulled Monika up.

Monika let the man pull her towards him. When she was very close to him she stepped very hard on his right foot with the sharp heel of her left foot. The man cried out in pain and let go of her.

Monika turned and ran into the crowds at the fair. It was hard to run fast as there were lots of people there now. She looked back over her shoulder. The bearded man and his friend were close behind her. In front of her there was a queue of people waiting for something. Monika pushed her way to the front of the queue. Then she saw what they were waiting in line for – it was the Big Wheel.

Monika jumped onto one of the Big Wheel's seats. A man asked for her ticket. 'My friends will pay,' Monika replied, pointing to the two men behind her.

The Big Wheel started and Monika rose up in the air above the Feira Popular. The wheel stopped. Monika looked down and saw the two men getting on to a seat behind her. The wheel started again and Monika went up even higher. She could see the lights of Maputo beneath her.

But now Monika didn't have time to enjoy the view. There was a loud bang and a singing noise as something hit the seat she was on. Monika looked back. One of Vitjord's men had a gun. He was shooting at her.

'I can't stay here,' Monika thought. 'I must do something.'

Carefully she stood up on her seat and caught hold of one of the metal bars above it. Then she lifted herself up on to the next seat. There was another shot. The Big Wheel stopped and Monika looked down. A crowd of people were looking up at her. Monika could see Cabinda's worried face in the crowd. The wheel started again. Vitjord's men were now above Monika. Monika stood up again and jumped to the next seat in front of her. Her hands moved and she almost fell. There was a cry from the crowd. Now she was two seats away from the men and they couldn't see her.

The wheel continued to turn and Monika was near the bottom. As the ground came closer she got ready and then jumped. She landed with a bump and fell to the ground. The wheel continued to turn carrying the men up again.

'Are you all right, Monika?' Cabinda asked.

Monika looked up at him and smiled. 'Yes, I think so,' she said. 'Look, I've got an idea. Can you ask the man to stop the wheel and leave those two high up in the air?'

Cabinda laughed and went over to the man who was working the wheel. Monika got to her feet and waited. Cabinda came back with a big smile on his face.

'That's OK,' he said. 'He'll keep them up there for ten minutes – enough time for us to get away in a taxi!'

The next morning Cabinda helped Monika get a ticket for the Sunday flight. She spent the rest of Saturday sightseeing with Cabinda and Amelia in Maputo.

At the airport on Sunday Monika thanked Cabinda and Amelia for everything they had done for her and promised to come back and visit them soon.

Two hours later the Air France 747 took off. Monika closed her eyes and fell asleep. She dreamed she was walking on the wing of the plane. When she woke the plane was landing. 'Where am I?' she thought. 'We can't be in Paris already.' She saw a sign on an airport building – Jan Smuts Airport, Johannesburg.

'Oh, no!' Monika thought. 'I'm back in South Africa!'

Chapter 12 *Help! I'm dying!*

Monika looked out of the window of the Air France 747 in surprise. She had thought she was on a flight to Paris, not Johannesburg. Then she heard the pilot's voice. 'We're staying in Johannesburg for forty-five minutes to take on more passengers. You may stay on the plane if you wish.'

'Oh, yes,' Monika thought. 'I'm staying on the plane. I don't want to meet Vitjord again!'

The flight took off for Paris on time and arrived early on Monday morning. Monika then took an SAS plane to Stockholm and was in Anders Blom's office in the Old Town by lunchtime.

'So that's what happened,' Monika said as she finished telling Blom about her adventures in South Africa and Mozambique.

'Well done!' Blom said. He had Monika's cassette from the Carlton in his hand. 'I've listened to this with great interest. What we must do now is clear. First of all, we must make sure that Carlsson is safe. We don't want another shooting. Secondly, we must try and stop Vitjord getting the nuclear bomb.'

Monika nodded. 'When is Carlsson's meeting?' she asked.

'It's on Friday evening at the Strand Hotel,' Blom replied. 'We've been busy while you've been away. I'm sure that Millham United, the English football team, are part of this plan. They arrived in Gothenburg on the ferry from England on Sunday. Then they drove straight here to Stockholm and took the evening ferry to St Petersburg. They are staying in Russia for three days and playing a match in St Petersburg. Then they are returning to Stockholm by ferry, playing a match here on Friday, and going down to Gothenburg on Friday evening.'

Monika thought for a minute.

'How strange,' she said slowly. 'Why go by coach and ferry? Why don't Millham United fly to Russia?'

'Exactly!' Blom said with a smile. 'We have to find out what is so special about their coach. When they get back to Stockholm on Friday, I want you to search their coach. Now we've got three days to plan the security for Carlsson's meeting at the Strand.'

Monika spent the rest of the week working to make sure that no-one would shoot Carlsson. Everyone going into the Strand Hotel was going to be searched and all the rooms were being checked.

Meanwhile, Millham United were in Russia. Their ferry arrived in St Petersburg at four o'clock on Monday. The football team went to their hotel. Then the coach, with only Dixon and Worthington, the chairman and manager of the club, and Kent Nyström and Gunilla Lippich, the two young Swedes, drove out of St Petersburg on the road to Moscow. After about a hundred kilometres the coach turned off onto a side road. The side road ran through a forest. It was soon dark.

The coach stopped by a high wall, where someone was waiting for it. Big doors in the wall opened and the coach drove through. Two men in hats and long coats got into the coach.

Dixon gave them a very heavy sports bag. The men opened the bag and then smiled. There was something shiny and yellow in the bag.

'The best South African gold,' Dixon said with a laugh.

The men in long coats took the heavy bag and put it in a black car. The others got off the coach. Then the men in long coats carried what looked like a very large heavy suitcase over to the coach from the car. Worthington opened a door in the side of the coach. The huge 'suitcase' was put in and the door was locked. Then the bus returned to St Petersburg.

Millham United played their match in St Petersburg and then took the ferry back to Stockholm as planned on Thursday evening. In Stockholm the team again stayed at the Strand.

Monika and a group of twenty SMI agents followed Millham United everywhere in Stockholm. The SMI searched the team's hotel bedrooms. They listened to the team's phone calls. They tape-recorded the team's conversations.

'Nothing,' Monika told Blom. 'We can't find anything. They're just a football team. There is one strange thing though. We can't search the coach. There are always people with it.'

'Don't give up,' said Blom. 'Stay with them until they leave the city. Then join me at the Strand. Carlsson's meeting is at eight o'clock tonight.'

Monika didn't give up. She watched Millham United play at the Stadion, the 1912 Olympic stadium in

Stockholm. Millham United won 3–2. The police locked up twelve Millham fans. Then the team left the Strand Hotel to go to Gothenburg in their coach.

'Nothing,' Monika told Blom. They were in his office. 'We found nothing. But we couldn't get near the coach.'

'We will,' Blom said. 'I've got an idea.'

'But how?' Monika asked. 'They are on their way to Gothenburg now and they're leaving Sweden in the morning.'

'I'll tell you on the way to the meeting,' Blom replied with a quick smile. 'Let's think about Carlsson now.'

It was six o'clock when Blom and Monika got to the Strand Hotel. They were searched as they entered the hotel by an SMI man.

'Good,' Blom said. 'I told them to search everyone. We can't take any chances.'

The hotel was still partly full of tourists and businessmen. But the hotel's main restaurant was closed for the night for Carlsson's meeting. The restaurant was in the middle of the hotel. Blom and Monika went in and looked around. The restaurant didn't have a ceiling. Above the restaurant there were rows of windows going up six floors to a glass roof. A large tree grew in the middle of the restaurant. In front of the tree there was a long table with a microphone.

'We've checked all the rooms,' Blom said. 'And all the hotel guests and staff have been searched. There are no weapons here. Carlsson is safe.'

In room 615 on the sixth floor a man was very busy. He had checked into the hotel the day before. Security men had searched his bag and his guitar case. But now he took a shiny electric guitar out of the case. He started working to turn the guitar into a crossbow. By half past seven he was ready. His guitar had become a weapon able to kill a man at a hundred metres. He took out a heavy metal bolt and put it into the crossbow. Then he looked at his watch and sat and waited.

The window of the man's room looked down at the restaurant. People were arriving for Carlsson's meeting now, and the restaurant was filling up. There were more people than had been at the first meeting at the City Hall. The shooting of Carlsson had increased international interest in his idea. The man in room 615 waited.

By the restaurant door Monika and Blom waited.

At exactly eight o'clock a man in a dark suit came into the restaurant. It was Carlsson. Everyone stood up.

In room 615, the man opened the window a little. He picked up the crossbow, and looked down at the people in the restaurant.

Monika looked up at the windows above the restaurant. Something caught her eye. It was a bright light. She had seen a light like that before. Outside the City Hall at the Water Festival.

The man in room 615 stood at the window and held up the crossbow. Monika saw the light again. Then she saw the shiny guitar. She turned to Blom.

'There's someone at that window! I'm going up to see what it is,' Monika said. She ran up the stairs to the sixth floor. There were lots of doors. Which room was it? Monika tried to remember where the room was. She kicked open the door of room 613. Empty! Room 614. Empty!

In room 615 the man was ready to shoot. Then there was a loud crash as Monika kicked down the door. The man turned and pointed the crossbow at her. Monika threw herself across the room at the man. She crashed into his legs, knocking the crossbow, which fell to the floor. The man tried to push Monika away and hit her on the head with the side of his hand. Her hands let go of him for a moment and he threw her down to the floor.

Monika hit the floor with a bang. The man ran across the room to the door. Lying on the floor Monika picked up the crossbow.

'Stop,' she shouted. The man didn't stop. Monika shot him in the right leg with the crossbow and he fell to the floor by the door.

Monika got up and ran over to the man. He was lying face down. Monika turned him over with her foot. To her great surprise she knew who the man was. It was Bruce, the man she had met on the Mariella, the guitarist. His face was full of pain.

'I'm dying!' he cried. 'Help!'

Monika stopped for a moment. This was the man who had shot Carlsson. But this was also the man whose music she liked, the man she liked. She felt sorry for him. He was lying at her feet crying, with blood on his leg. He needed her help.

Monika got down beside Bruce. He looked at her in surprise. 'Please help me,' he said.

'You're not dying, so stop crying,' Monika said roughly. 'Who are you?'

'You know who I am,' Bruce said. 'And now I know who you are.'

'Why did you shoot Carlsson?' Monika asked.

No reply.

Monika got up and walked over to the crossbow. She picked it up and put another bolt in it. Then she walked back and pointed the crossbow at Bruce's left leg.

'Answer my questions or I'll shoot,' she said.

Bruce looked at her. Then his face changed and became angry.

'Yes,' he said in a loud voice. 'I shot Carlsson at the City Hall. And tonight I was going to kill him.'

'But why?' Monika asked.

'For my father,' Bruce replied. 'My father wants Carlsson dead.'

'And who is your father?' Monika asked.

'You don't know him,' Bruce said. 'He's a great man. One day he will be the leader of my country. His name's Vitjord.'

Monika looked at Bruce in surprise. 'He's your father, is he? Vitjord?' she said.

'Yes,' Bruce replied. 'Do you know him?'

'Unfortunately, I do,' Monika said. She looked up as two SMI men ran into the room.

'Here's the man who shot Carlsson,' she said. 'He's hurt his leg. Take care of him.' She then threw the crossbow onto the bed and walked out of the room.

Chapter 13   *What are you doing here?*

Monika walked slowly down the stairs to the restaurant. Her mind was full of thoughts. Why did she do this job? She had just shot a man she liked. A few days before she had danced with him, not knowing that he had tried to kill Carlsson. But she was pleased she had saved Carlsson.

Blom was waiting for her outside. She told him what had happened. He listened and nodded.

'You're the best agent we have,' he said. Monika smiled. It was as if her parents were saying how good she was.

'Now,' Blom went on. 'Do you remember what I told you on the way here?'

'Yes,' Monika replied with a smile. 'I'm flying to Gothenburg. Tomorrow I'm going on the ferry to England. When the ship is at sea I am to search the coach.'

'Exactly,' Blom said. 'Because on a ferry no-one is allowed to stay with the cars and coaches. You will be able to search the coach with no-one there.'

'There's just one thing,' Monika said. 'What if something goes wrong?'

Blom smiled. 'Yes, I've thought of that. Twelve SMI agents will also be on the ferry with you. They are already in Gothenburg. Lars Nilsson is their leader. You know him, don't you?'

Monika nodded. She and Blom spent the rest of the evening at the Strand. Carlsson's meeting was a great success. He got the one billion dollars he needed to destroy the nuclear weapons. It was nearly midnight before Blom and Monika left the hotel.

'I've just thought of something,' Monika said. 'It's too late to get a plane to Gothenburg tonight!'

'Oh no, it isn't,' Blom replied. 'You're going on a military plane. And you'll be the only passenger!'

A car took Monika to a military airport and she was flown to Gothenburg. After a few hours sleep she went to the Skandiahamn, where the blue and white ferries left for England.

Lars Nilsson was waiting for her. He was tall with short grey hair. From the top of the harbour building Monika and Lars watched cars drive onto the ferry. The ship was called The Princess of Scandinavia and was long and thin. When the cars were on the ferry, the coaches were driven on.

'There it is,' Monika said. 'There's the Millham United coach.' She could see the driver and two other people on the coach.

'That's strange,' she said to Lars. 'There are three people on the coach. Usually all the passengers walk on and only the driver stays with the coach.'

Monika and Lars left the harbour building and went on to the ferry. They met the other SMI agents in a quiet room, near the floor where the coaches were parked. The room was full of TV screens.

'Right, men,' Lars said. 'This is the plan. Monika is going to search the coach alone. We will be able to see what is happening on these TV screens. There are lots of cameras on the car and coach floor of the ferry. When the ferry leaves the harbour, the doors to the car and coach floor will be locked, and no-one will be allowed in.'

'Except me!' Monika said brightly. It was good to work with other people and not always to be on her own.

'Any questions?' Lars asked. 'No? OK. It's just a question of waiting now.'

They watched the passengers leave their cars on the TV screens. They saw the Millham United coach driver check the coach carefully, and lock it. Monika wondered what had happened to the other two people on the coach. Perhaps they had already got off.

Half an hour later Monika could hear the noise of the engines as the ship started. The SMI agents watched the TV screens. There were still people getting bags from the cars. Monika waited.

Two hours later Monika was ready. Lars helped her open the locked door to the car and coach floor.

'Good luck!' he said.

Monika walked quietly over to the Millham United coach. She had lots of keys with her, and the first thing she did was to open the driver's door and get in. It was empty. She got out again, and looked at the coach. It was very high and on the side there were two big doors. She opened the first door and stepped in. Suitcases. The second door would not open at first. Then a key worked and the door opened. Monika looked into blackness. There seemed to be nothing there. She climbed in. There was plenty of room for her to stand but she could see nothing. She put her hands out in front of her. Then she touched something. It was warm. It was a person!

Suddenly two hands held her throat. She couldn't

breathe. Her head was banged against the side of the coach again and again. 'Help!' she thought. 'Lars won't be able to see me on the TV screens.'

She tried to hit the person holding her. By chance she hit something on the wall, and a light came on. She could see who the person in the coach was. It was Vitjord! He had been hiding inside the coach. Vitjord let go of Monika's throat. Then he hit her across the face. She fell to the floor of the coach. Vitjord kicked her hard.

'Now, my little Swedish friend,' Vitjord said. 'What are you doing here? Have you come to see my toy? Well, have a look at it before I kill you.'

Vitjord pressed something and part of the floor opened. Monika could see a large green box like a suitcase. There were Russian letters on the box.

'This is my little toy,' Vitjord said. 'And you're not going to take it away from me. This bomb is going to make me leader of South Africa.'

Monika looked at him. There was nothing she could do. Lars couldn't see her on the TV screens.

'Now,' Vitjord said, taking out a knife, 'I'm going to kill you.'

'Stop!' a voice said.

Monika recognised the voice. It was Chapman! He had come to save her!

'Don't kill her!' Chapman was standing behind Vitjord. 'Don't kill her yet,' Chapman said. 'Let's make her talk first.'

Monika understood now. Chapman wasn't going to save her. He was working with Vitjord. He and Vitjord were the people she had seen on the coach at Gothenburg when it drove onto the ferry. Chapman was also the person who had told Vitjord that Monika was in Johannesburg.

'What are you doing here?' she asked Chapman.

He looked down at her and then kicked her in the side of the head. 'I ask the questions here, my stupid little Swede. As a matter of fact, Mr Vitjord and I are old friends. We are working together for a new white South Africa. Now, how did you know the bomb was here?'

Monika didn't say anything. Vitjord touched her face with his knife.

'Answer, now!' Vitjord said as his face came close to hers.

'The police have got your son, Vitjord. We know he tried to murder Carlsson,' said Monika.

For a second Vitjord thought about this. Monika moved quickly, bringing her knee up between Vitjord's legs. He cried in pain and dropped the knife.

Monika got to her feet and turned towards Chapman. He had a gun in his hand. Monika moved sideways towards the knife. She picked it up quickly and threw it at Chapman. It hit him in the shoulder and he fell backwards out of the coach. Monika jumped after him, but Chapman was waiting. He hit her across the face with the gun and Monika fell to the floor. Chapman raised the gun. There was a mad look in his eyes.

'Kill her! Kill her!' shouted Vitjord from the coach.

Suddenly there was a loud explosion, and the air filled with smoke. People in black with guns ran towards the coach. There was a bang as Chapman fired his gun. Monika felt a pain in her shoulder. Her eyes closed. Everything went dark.

Monika opened her eyes again. She was in hospital. Blom was by her bed.

'OK?' he asked.

Monika smiled. 'I think so,' she said. 'What happened?'

'Lars Nilsson saw Chapman fall out of the coach with a gun in his hand. Lars and his men threw smoke bombs at the coach. Chapman shot you in the shoulder. You were very lucky.'

'And Vitjord?' Monika asked.

'Lars and the others caught both Vitjord and Chapman.' Blom replied. 'And they've got the bomb. The danger is over. The ferry had to return to Gothenburg. The police here are questioning the Millham United people now. But how are you? How do you feel?'

'Well,' Monika said, and thought for a moment. She thought about Vitjord and his son, Bruce. She thought about Cabinda and his wife, who had been so good to her. She thought about being on top of the Big Wheel, and then about Chapman who had double crossed her and almost killed her.

Then she smiled and said: 'You know, ever since this business started I've felt like I've been standing on the wing of a plane.'